MILAN

TRAVEL GUIDE

2024-2025

Your Personalized Milan Adventure Starts Now.

MABEL MARTIN

TABLE OF CONTENT

MAP OF MILAN

INTRODUCTION

As I sit down to recount the marvels of Milan, my heart flutters with the same exhilaration that swept over me when I first stepped into this city of boundless charm and hidden treasures. Milan, often hailed as the world's fashion capital, unfolded before me like a meticulously crafted tapestry, woven with threads of ancient history, avant-garde design, and an undying spirit of innovation. This travel guide is my ode to Milan, a city that captivated my soul and transformed the way I perceive the world.

My journey began under the watchful gaze of the Madonnina, perched atop the majestic Duomo di Milano. As I gazed upon this marvel of gothic architecture, its marble façade gleaming in the sunlight, I felt a profound connection to the centuries of human endeavor and devotion encapsulated within its spires. The piazza, pulsating with the rhythm of city life, was a prelude to the myriad experiences that lay ahead.

Wandering through the Galleria Vittorio Emanuele II, I marveled at the opulent architecture and the whisper of footsteps on its mosaic floors, telling tales of the past. Each turn revealed a blend of luxury and legacy, from the haute couture boutiques to the historic cafes where intellectuals once debated the future of Italy. Milan, I realized, is a city that honors its past while boldly striding into the future.

The Sforzesco Castle offered a different whisper of history, its red-brick battlements and serene courtyards a testament to Milan's tumultuous past and artistic heritage. As I delved deeper into the city, the Brera District, with its bohemian allure, captured my imagination. The artistry of the Brera Art Gallery, the enchanting streets, and the vibrant market—it all felt like stepping into a living canvas, each brushstroke a narrative of beauty and inspiration.

Yet, Milan's soul is not confined to its monuments and museums. It thrives in the every day, in the laughter that fills the Navigli canals as the sun sets, painting the waters with hues of gold and amber. It's in the aroma of freshly brewed coffee wafting through the air, in the warmth of a Milanese smile, and in the clink of glasses as friends gather to share an aperitivo, embracing the joy of the moment.

My journey through Milan was not merely a voyage across a city but an exploration of the human spirit's capacity to create, preserve, and transform. I witnessed a city that vibrates with the energy of fashion weeks and design fairs, yet remains grounded in the timeless beauty of its cathedrals and piazzas. Milan taught me that beauty is not just to be observed but to be lived, in the rush of the metro, the tranquility of the parks, and the chatter of the markets.

To those who dream of visiting Milan, this guide is your gateway to a city that promises not just to show you its wonders but to offer you a piece of its heart. Milan is an experience, a feeling, a memory that lingers long after you've left its cobblestone streets behind. It's a reminder that every moment is an opportunity to find beauty, to seek inspiration, and to live with passion.

So, embark on this journey with me, through the pages of this guide, into the heart of Milan. Let us wander, discover, and fall in love with this extraordinary city together.

OVERVIEW OF MILAN

The capital of Lombardy, Milan, is home to 1.3 million people. With a variety of industries, it is the biggest industrial city in Italy. Milan draws tourists from all over the world because of its historic city core, which is home to palazzos and other tall, beautiful buildings.

HISTORY

Milan was established in 400 BC against the Etruscans, by Gauls.

Around 222 B.C. Rome invaded and conquered the city. Following the Edict of Tolerance toward Christianity in 313 A.D., several churches were constructed, and the first bishop was appointed. Because of his fame, Ambrogio's church was renamed the Ambrosian Church on December 7, which is Sant'Ambrogio Day. The Visconti family, aristocrats from Bergamo, Cremona, Piacenza, Brescia, and Parma, ruled in 1300 and ushered in a time of luxury and pride for the city. After being finished in 1386, the Duomo came to represent Milan.

After years of conflict with Florence and Venice, the Sforza family took control of the Visconti dynasty and the Castle, allowing Milan to finally achieve peace. The city saw the beginning of the blossoming of the arts, sciences, and literature under the Sforza duchy. Leonardo da Vinci and "il Bramante " were invited to Ludovico il Moro (Ludovico Sforza) court.

GEOGRAPHY AND CLIMATE

Milan is situated in Northern Italy on the low-lying Padan Plain and is encircled by mountains. Its climate is mostly Mediterranean, with hot, bright summers and chilly, rainier winters. Due to the geography and summer heat, it may be prone to intense fog. Travelers often feel that the best seasons to visit are spring and autumn since they escape the crowds and the heat. It only takes a few kilometers to leave the city and you'll find yourself surrounded by typical Italian country views, such as olive trees, cypress trees, and vineyards. If you'd like to travel a little farther, the renowned Lakes district is practically right outside your door, providing a breathtaking view of enormous lakes framed by stunning mountains. The population of Milan's central region is around 1.3 million, but when you include the surrounding metropolitan area, this number quadruples.

CLIMATE

Italy has a mostly Mediterranean climate, with hot, dry weather in the south and alpine conditions in the far north. Milan has a foggy, mild winter with temperatures between 0 and 8 degrees Celsius. Summertime temperatures range from 14 to 29 degrees and may be quite humid with brief thunderstorms. The temperature ranges from 6 to 18 degrees from March to April. They range from 6 to 17 degrees from October to November.

CULTURE AND ART

Milan has always been a powerful and affluent city. It has historically been home to several renowned artists and offers a unique assortment of churches, buildings, and monuments. The Renaissance brought forth a revolution in art and culture that greatly influenced the neoclassical era. Milan is home to a wide variety of structures, memorials, and museums. The Cathedral, the third-largest cathedral in the world, is the most well-known place of worship.

Overall, it is made of marble and has enormous statues, arches, pillars, and pinnacles. You may be able to get an amazing view of the city from the roof. Between 1466 and 1490, Santa Maria delle Grazie was constructed, and Bramante rebuilt it. One of Leonardo da Vinci's most well-known paintings, "The Last Supper," is located in the Refectory. Milan is home to some historic palazzos, one of which is the Royal Palace, or Palazzo Reale, which is situated on Piazza Duomo's southern edge. One of Milan's symbols is the Sforza Castle, which together with the Madonnina and the Galleria Vittorio Emanuele II are just a few reasons to come.

TRANSPORTATION

GETTING TO MILAN

Italy's northern city of Milan is easily reached by car and airplane. With three sizable international airports, it serves as Italy's main entry point. The easiest and quickest ways to go from where you're departing to Milan are as follows:

By Air

Since low-cost airlines from Europe began operating there, Milan and Lombardy have grown in popularity as travel destinations in Italy. Milan, the capital of Lombardy, is home to many beautiful towns and villages, as well as the Italian lakes. Each year, more than 50 million people arrive and depart from Milan's airports.

Departing from the US.

Finding nonstop flights to Milan from the United States is difficult. Still, a lot of international airports, such as Chicago (ORD), Los Angeles (LAX), Boston (BOS), Houston (IAH), and Dallas (DFW), have one-stop flights. These don't have to be expensive. We advise traveling via New York for a connecting flight to Milan if you do not live very close to an international airport. At the moment, Delta Airlines and Alitalia are the only airlines operating direct flights from New York JFK to Milan (Malpensa Airport). Additionally, United Airlines offers nonstop service between Newark and Milan. Malpensa Airport is the destination for all US flights.

Departing from Australia

Emirates, Singapore Airlines, Etihad Airways, and Virgin Australia are the airlines that fly to Milan the most often from Australia. These depart from Perth, Brisbane, Sydney, and Melbourne. Typically, flights last between 23 and 30 hours.

Departing from Europe

The following airlines are the most frequent visitors to Milan's airports if they are flying from the United Kingdom:

EasyJet: From Edinburgh, Glasgow, London Gatwick, London Luton, and Manchester, EasyJet operates direct flights to Milan.

Ryanair: Ryanair is based in Manchester, East Midlands, Edinburgh (very few flights), and London Stansted.

Flybe: Direct flights from Birmingham, Manchester, Cardiff, and Hannover are offered by this airline.

British Airways

The Alitalia

Train

The most convenient way to get through Italy if you want to visit the nation while you're there is by train. By train, the trip from Venice to Milan takes two hours. Three hours are needed from Rome. There are slower, less expensive trains if you're not in a hurry.

Bus

If you're on a tight budget, you may opt to use the bus rather than the train to tour the whole country.

GETTING AROUND

The most convenient way to get to Milan is to use the ATM, an effective and reasonably priced public transportation system. This tram, bus, and subway system is extensive and reasonably priced. Another good option is metered taxis, although if you just use them for transit, they may become expensive. You may just want to walk if your hotel is close to the Duomo, which is regarded as the city's center, since there are plenty of other attractions and amenities only blocks away. Like other major European cities, Milan has expensive traffic and little parking, so driving is not recommended.

Milan is served by two airports: Milan Linate Airport (LIN), which is just about 5 miles from the city center, and handles fewer flights (mostly local, but some European), and Milan Malpensa Airport (MXP), which is a little more than 30 miles northeast, welcomes most international aircraft. You may use the Malpensa Express, which costs 20 euros, or about $22, to go from Milan Malpensa to the city center (for a round-trip ticket). No train travels into the city from Linate. Take the No. 73 bus into the downtown instead. Another, although expensive, option is taxis. Depending on where you are in Linate, you should budget between 40 and 80 euros (about $47.85 and $95.70) and 110 euros (around $121) to go to the city center.

Advice: You should visit Milan's trams, some of which are over a century old. Take tram No. 1 in front of Sforza Castle to view La Scala, the Arco della Pace, and other sights along one of Milan's most attractive streets.

Public Transport

Milan's bus, tram, and metro systems make getting about the city affordable and easy. A single-trip urban ticket costs 2.20 euros (about $2.40) and covers travel just inside Milan's metropolitan area, not the suburbs. Tickets are only good for ninety minutes after purchase and cost the same for the metro, bus, and tram. If you want to use the ATM often while there, you may purchase a book of ten tickets for 19.50 euros (about $21). You may use your phone, credit or debit card, or contactless payment alternatives in Milan's metro stations, trams, and buses to make payments on the go. Trams and buses are not to be concerned about; the subway drops down passengers right in front of several well-known sites, such as the Duomo and the Santa Maria delle Grazie, which is home to "The Last Supper." Although the subway is open late, tickets must be purchased after midnight for them to be valid during that time. During the midweek breaks, many night buses run on Fridays, Saturdays, and Sundays. Subway stations sell tickets for all ATM transport options.

Cab

In this city, taxis are commonplace and reasonably priced for an occasional journey, but using them often might become expensive quickly. The base charge is about 3.90 euros (approximately $4), and each additional kilometer you drive will cost you 1.28 euros ($1.30). Taxis are available at many locations across the city, particularly close to popular sights and convenient lodging. It is not possible to hail a taxi from the street here. Taxis with licenses are white.

Automobile

You could be considering taking a car to Milan since Florence is around 3.5 hours distant and Rome is about 6 hours away. Still, driving is usually a hassle in the city.

There are areas of the city that are off-limits to cars due to environmental concerns, gas prices are high (over $5 per gallon), and parking is difficult. Car rentals are available at the LIN and MXP airports, if necessary.

On Foot

You cannot walk through the whole of Milan since it is around 70 square miles in size. But the best way to see Milan, like with many other European towns, is to take a walk. It is best to stick to walking if you are at or close to the Duomo. Famous locations are about a mile apart in this area. Additionally, you'll come across a ton of eateries and establishments that you should check out.

ACCOMMODATION

LUXURY HOTELS

1. Milan Armani Hotel

Situated in the center of Milan's well-known Quadrilatero della Moda, the Armani Hotel Milano offers unparalleled accessibility to the city's upscale clothing stores and historical landmarks.

This hotel, which includes 95 rooms and suites with every detail meticulously designed by Giorgio Armani personally, embodies the Armani lifestyle and design philosophy. The accommodations are the pinnacle of comfort and elegance, complete with rich fabrics, bespoke furniture, and cutting-edge amenities.

Cost: The cost of a standard room varies according to the season and availability, starting at around €750 per night.

2. Milan Four Seasons Hotel

Nestled in a renovated 15th-century convent, the Four Seasons Hotel Milano offers a sophisticated haven in the bustling city center, conveniently close to the Duomo and Teatro alla Scala.

The hotel has 118 elegantly furnished guestrooms and suites that seamlessly combine contemporary comforts with classic Italian design. Visitors may unwind in the hotel's top-notch spa, dine in the exquisite La Veranda restaurant, and take in the tranquil enclosed courtyard, which is a haven of peace.

Cost: The starting nightly fee for a superior room is around €1,100; however, the exact price may vary based on the season and the kind of lodging selected.

3. Oriental Mandarin Milan

The Mandarin Oriental Milan is conveniently located near the famed La Scala theater, at the intersection of Milan's economic, fashion, and cultural sectors. This makes it the perfect starting point for guests to explore the city.

The hotel's 104 tastefully decorated rooms and suites blend the brand's eastern heritage with Milanese design. Antonio Citterio, a renowned designer, combined modernity and elegance in his ideas for the rooms. A superb dining experience is also ensured by the hotel's two Michelin-starred restaurants, Seta and the more relaxed Mandarin Bar & Bistrot.

Cost: Depending on the season and style of lodging, standard accommodations start at around €800 per night.

4. Grand Spa and Hotel Palazzo Parigi

With a variety of galleries, shops, and cafés close by, Palazzo Parigi, which is situated in the well-known Brera area, offers guests a taste of Milan's cultural scene while being just a short stroll from the city's historic center.

This opulent hotel and grand spa has 98 spacious rooms and suites designed to provide guests with the ultimate comfort and style. The hotel's magnificent garden or the Milanese skyline may be seen from the rooms, which are tastefully decorated with fine artwork. The hotel's Grand Spa is a roomy wellness haven with an indoor pool, a fitness center, and a selection of treatments.

Cost: The starting rate for a deluxe room is around €600 per night; however, this might vary based on the details of the booking and the time of year.

BUDGET HOTELS

1. B&B Hotel Sant'Ambrogio in Milan

The Duomo di Milano and the Sforzesco Castle, two of Milan's main attractions, are easily accessible from this hotel thanks to its handy location in a quiet neighborhood next to the Sant'Ambrogio Metro Station. Modern and comfortable accommodations are offered by the B&B Hotel Milano Sant'Ambrogio, which has amenities for both leisure and business travelers. Modern furnishings like free Wi-Fi, air conditioning, and a flat-screen TV are included in the rooms. The hotel is a great choice for anyone looking for a discount in the center of Milan because of its peaceful atmosphere and helpful personnel.

Cost: Depending on the season and availability, a standard double room might cost anywhere from €70 to €90 per night.

2. Berna Hotel

Situated only a short stroll from Milan Central Station, Hotel Berna provides excellent access to the extensive public transportation system in the city, facilitating tourists' exploration of Milan's many neighborhoods and attractions.

The Hotel Berna is notable for its excellent customer service, immaculate surroundings, and comfortable lodging. Every room has a minibar, free high-speed Wi-Fi, and other modern amenities. It is also soundproofed. The hotel also offers a large breakfast buffet with a variety of delectable and fresh options to provide a proper start to the day.

Cost: The starting nightly charge for a classic room is around €90, however, the exact amount may vary depending on the time of year and the booking conditions.

3. Bello Ostello

The active city heart of Milan is well situated for Ostello Bello, which is just a short distance from both the lively Navigli area and the iconic Duomo. For those who want to fully immerse themselves in Milanese culture and history, this region is excellent.

Ostello Bello is a vibrant hostel that offers comfort, culture, and community—it's more than just a place to sleep. It is appropriate for different types of travelers since it provides a range of hotel options, from private rooms to communal dormitories. Shared kitchens, a rooftop terrace, and regular social events are available to visitors, creating a warm setting where people can mingle and exchange stories.

Cost: Depending on the season and specific booking conditions, a bed in a shared dorm may cost as little as €35 per night, while private rooms can cost up to €80 per night.

VACATION RENTALS

1. Navigli Charming Apartment

This lovely apartment is located in the center of the Navigli district, which is well-known for its vibrant nightlife, boutiques, and canal-side cafés. It places guests in one of Milan's most picturesque and busy areas. For those who want to fully immerse themselves in the local way of life and take in Milan's renowned aperitivo scene, this is the ideal location.

Perfect for singles or couples, the beautifully furnished one-bedroom Navigli Charming Apartment is a great place to stay. It has a modern bathroom, a well-appointed kitchen, and a comfortable living area, all designed with an emphasis on comfort and elegance. Ample natural light and a view of the bustling street below are made possible by the large windows.

Cost: Depending on the time of year and duration of stay, rates may vary from around €120 per night to €240.

2. Brera Artistic Studio

Located in Milan's hip Brera neighborhood, this studio apartment is close to both Sempione Park's verdant surroundings and the renowned Pinacoteca di Brera art museum. The area is also well-known for its bohemian charm, chic shops, and excellent dining options.

For art lovers and those looking for a blend of tradition and modern Milanese life, the Brera Artistic Studio is an excellent substitute. This little but stylish apartment has a cozy sleeping area, a tiny kitchenette for preparing meals, and a private bathroom, all decorated with artistic accents that pay homage to the local way of life.

Cost: Depending on the dates of booking and the length of stay, the nightly fee for this studio begins at around €100.

3. New Loft close to Duomo

This contemporary apartment is the ideal starting point for exploring Milan's historical sites and cutting-edge shops since it is located only a short stroll from the well-known Duomo di Milano and the bustling shopping district.

Travelers who value urban aesthetics will love this loft's clean architecture and contemporary facilities. It has an open-concept living area with a mezzanine bedroom, dining area, lounge area, and fully functional kitchen. The room is flooded with light from the floor-to-ceiling windows, which also provide a stunning view of the metropolitan skyline.

Cost: The starting rate for this loft is €150 per night. The duration of the rental term and the season might have an impact on rates.

FOOD AND DRINK

TRADITIONAL MILANESE CUISINE

When in Rome, you might do as the Romans do, but in Milan, you've got to ingest what the Milanese eat.

1. Minestrone Milanese

Who needs GPS when you have a minestrone? Some say that a few tastes of the broth will tell you precisely where you are on the peninsula. The rice is prepared in a delightful if not particularly noteworthy broth. Served heated in the winter and chilled in the summer, this broth is your best option for a few servings of vegetables, which don't feature prominently in most traditional Milanese restaurants.

2. Osso Bucco

Meat, meat and more meat: that's what you'll be consuming in Milan if you go for the region's iconic dishes (sorry, herbivores). Ossobuco, which translates to "bone with a hole," is one of two meat heroes (cotoletta being the other, see below for more on that) you'll find at most traditional restaurants. Braised in a concoction of onions, carrots, celery, white wine and bouillon, the crosscut veal shank is fork-tender and dissolves in the mouth. The jelly-like marrow at the center of the bone elevates this dish from merely delectable to divine. It's often served with risotto alla Milanese or polenta.

Where to get it: Osteria dell'Acquabella in Porta Romana, a basic, family-run spot that relies almost exclusively on Milanese culinary traditions, consistently turns out an exceptional ossobuco.

3. Panettone

There are many legends about the precise origins of this Christmas fruitcake, and almost all of them point to Milan as its origin. Panettone is everywhere during the holiday season, with cases heaped high in bakeries and filling up entire sections in supermarkets, and many people buy it as a gift for friends and family: nothing distributes a bit of joy like a slice of this pillowy, sweet bread and a glass of prosecco. But you may be astonished to find out that there are patisserie shops that bake panettone all year round; these locations have mastered the notoriously difficult bread, which is packed full of large pieces of candied citrus and raisins.

Where to get it: One of the finest locations for panettone is Pasticceria Cucchi, an opulent store on Corso Genova that seems delightfully preserved in time.

4. Cassoeula

A nourishing pork and cabbage stew, cassoeula typically shows up on menus during the harsher months, when all you want is a dish of scalding hot deliciousness. This is one of those head-to-tail Italian recipes – in addition to sausage and cabbage, less noble pig parts like the head, feet, ears and more are flung into the stew. It's traditionally consumed on January 17, the feast day of Saint Anthony the Abbot, fittingly the patron saint of swine and butchers, among other things.

Where to get it: One of the finest locations in Milan offering cassoeula year-round is Don Lisander, an old-school restaurant that borders Brera and Quadrilatero Della Moda, two neighborhoods north of the Duomo.

5 Polenta

If not prepared correctly, polenta might turn out to be bland and uninspired, which could be the reason for its unfavorable image. It can become too gelatinous or bake into an extremely stiff loaf. However, when cooked correctly, boiling cornmeal, often known as cornmeal porridge, is among the best comfort meals available. To celebrate the importance of polenta in Italian culture, several associations were established in the 18th and 19th centuries, demonstrating how passionate Northern Italians are about their dish.

Where to purchase it: Although polenta is often served as an accompaniment to main courses of meat and stew, Al Cantinone, a restaurant close to the Duomo, has some excellent appetizers.

6. Gorgonzola

The region was long known for producing cheese, especially soft cheese; documents from Empress Maria Theresa's court in the 18th century are said to have said that the region should be utilized as pasture for dairy cattle. These days, the unskimmed milk used to make blue cheese is produced across northern Italy, mainly in the provinces of Piedmont and Lombardy. There are two varieties of gorgonzola: the richer, creamier dolce (meaning "sweet") and the pungent, peppery piccante (meaning "spicy").

Where to get it: Try the Italian cheese platter at Asso di Fiori ("ace of cheese"), or go for the expanded menu that includes cheeses soaked in wine and cold meats.

7. The Piadina

Originating in the modern Emilia-Romagna area, the piadina has taken over Milan's lunch crowd, where it is stuffed to the brim with cheeses, meats, and sometimes vegetables. People make short work of the piadinas, relishing the melted cheese inside before it freezes, even in more sophisticated settings where they are not nearly as laden with sauces.

BEST DINING DISTRICTS

Milan's food culture is cosmopolitan, lively, and constantly on top of the newest trends, perfectly capturing the fast-paced spirit of the city. With fresh ideas to keep up with the diverse population of the city, traditional Italian foods continue to be at the forefront of each recipe.

Whatever your taste, Milan has something to offer you, from world-class Michelin-starred restaurants to quirky pop-ups and hidden pizzerias.

Here are a few of Milan's best restaurant' locations:

Brera Porta Nuova

District of Porta Genova - Corso Como - Portello

Brera

The fine art college that was converted to a gallery in the 18th century makes Brera one of Milan's creative hubs. Its quirky stores, hidden cafés, and cobblestone lanes add to its charm.

Brera is a gastronomic haven as well as a fashion attraction. There are a plethora of eateries in the vicinity to try.

Regarding regional food:

Niko Romito, the restaurateur

The Food Sette Cucina Urbana is saved by God.

Rovello 18, Bisco

Il Kaimano

Try these if fish is what you're craving:

Brera's Osteria

Il Cestino Consolare Trattoria Torre di Pisa

For real pizza from Italy: Pacifico Momus

The Brera Lievità Pizzacoteca

Follow the Milanese's lead. Here, take pleasure in a little refreshment or an aperitivo:

Tibi Provençal Bistro

Mercato Pandenus La Tartina

La Casa Iberica

N'Ombra de Vin

The nearest rail stations to Brera are Lanza (M2 line) and Montenapoleone (M3 line) metro stations.

Porta Nuova

In every way, Porta Nuova embodies Milan's modern spirit. This district is home to some of Italy's most notable architectural wonders. It is home to the Palazzo

Lombardia, the regional government seat of Lombardy, as well as two of the city's tallest attractions, the Bosco Verticale (Vertical Forest) and Torre Pelli (Pelli Tower).

There are several options here if you're strolling around Porta Nuova has stirred up an appetite. The ever-evolving culinary culture in the neighborhood offers many options, whether you're craving gourmet, international, or genuine Milanese cuisine.

These are some of the best restaurants serving foreign food, ranging from Asia to South America and all points in between:

Thank you very much, Le Vrai Vin Han Long, No. 29 Babies

Milan surely knows how to wow if you've been craving real Italian pizza.

The COSÍ of Nàpiz is Antonino Esposito

N'ata - Pizza Expressions

Da Cecco

Would you want to try some of the classics, such as the Cassöeula, Ossobuco (cross-cut veal shanks cooked with vegetables in liquid), or traditional risotto? This is where you should go:

Italian Risotteria

The Varrone Griglia

Joia Ristorante Berton Il Liberty

The Verme Osteria in Ratanà

The nearest rail station to Porta Nuova is the Milano Repubblica train and metro station (M3 line), as well as the Turati metro stop (M3 line).

Corso Como

You are not going to want to miss some of the best gastronomic experiences that this fascinating micro-world in the center of Milan has to offer. The neighborhood is a fusion of styles, ranging from futuristic, almost abstract urbanization to early 20th-century architecture.

Corso Como is also well known for being a luxury shopping destination, with its magnificent haute couture ateliers and upscale stores. You may arrange a day full of fashion events and end the day with dinner at one of its unique eateries. Beyond that, things don't get much better.

The best cafés in the neighborhood are these:

10 Corso Como Café

Executive Lounge Pixel

Loolapaloosa Novecento Café

Pitbull Coffee

If you like customs, you must visit these restaurants:

everybody the Rocking Horse Isola

Sciatt Porter, A.

My Garba Bistrot

The Varrone Griglia

And why not try some food from other Italian areas while you're in Milan? Because of the great geographical diversity of Italy's cuisine, each place you visit seems like you're in a different section of the nation.

Restaurant in the Langhe Kitchen

The Pompero

The closest rail station is the Garibaldi train and metro station, which is a minute's walk away (M3 and M5 lines).

District of Portello

One of Milan's emerging neighborhoods is Portello, which is situated on the city's northwest edge. The neighborhood, which takes its name from the street Strada del Portello, is well-known for being the center of the car industry, having formerly housed the headquarters of Fiat and Alfa Romeo.

This place has a very diverse food culture. Traditional pizzerias, elegant dining for special events, and casual trattorias are just a few options. Some of the best restaurants to eat in this area of the city have been compiled by us.

Time for pizza? Make sure to keep an eye out for these pizzerias that you can eat in or take out:

Romantica Milan Amabile Piazza Portello

The Best Pizza Restaurant in Town

Here, the mangia

Visit these classic trattoria and restaurants for indigenous cuisine:

Portello Residence Ristorante Iper Risto

The Factory of the Gusti

The Two Sisters of the Rest Stop Paradise

Would you want espresso to finish? These are the best places in the area:

fervor for coffee

Mother Pilar Bar Modà Colonna Bar

The closest rail station is 16 16-minute' walk from either the M5 line's Portello metro station or the M1 line's QT8 metro station.

District of Porta Genova

One of the liveliest areas of the city is Porta Genova, which is situated between Navigli, the Darsena (dock), and Via Tortona. The neighborhood is worth visiting because of its fantastic nightlife, good shopping, and delicious Milanese trattorie.

There's no better place than Porta Genova to get quick street food, fresh Asian cuisine, or something a touch fancier.

To sample traditional Milanese food, go to:

The Taglio Scaletta

Meatball family

Binari Osteria

El Ganassin, El Barba Pedana

Milan's restaurant scene is diverse and multi-ethnic, with many eateries from various parts of Italy. Among the best in the vicinity of Porta Genova are:

Giordano's Acquasala Restaurant, a Bolognese restaurant called Trinacria Osteria Fiorentina

Milano Porta Genova rail and metro station (M3 line) is the closest train station.

CAFE AND COFFEE CULTURE

While a new wave of cafés in Milan is putting their unique touch on a time-honored recipe, other establishments have been serving espresso since the 19th century. These are the locations you won't want to miss, whether you're looking for a real taste of the city or just a fix of coffee. Pasticceria Marchesi

Milan would be difficult to imagine without Pasticceria Marchesi at its heart. Established in 1824 and managed by families for many generations, the esteemed establishment was acquired by the Prada Group in 2014 and now operates three locations around the city along with a branch in Mayfair, London. It's easy to see why: the exquisitely packed sugar-coated almonds and cremini are made with the highest quality components and meticulous attention to detail. The café at Via Monte Napoleone 9 boasts pistachio-hued décor and matching velvet couches where you can live out all your Instagram dreams. After that, you can recover in one of the top boutique hotels in the city, which is conveniently located. It's hard to choose which of the three places is the best.

Galleria's Camparino

This art nouveau gem is housed in the Galleria Vittorio Emanuele II emporium and is well-known for providing refreshments to composers Giuseppe Verdi and Arturo Toscanini after a night at the Scala opera venue. It's a traditional spot for a Spritz at the end of the day, although breakfast, lunch, and aperitivo are served there every day beginning at 8 a.m. Order a coffee at the bar, just as the Milanese do, and you'll be able to get a close-up look at the original wall mosaic by Angelo d'Andrea and the custom cabinets by Eugenio Quarti. Alternatively, take a seat outdoors in the plaza to get a front-row view of the Duomo.

Milano Pavé

When you purchase coffee in Milan, you usually have to stand at the counter and down an espresso without even taking off your overcoat. Pavé's retro furnishings and kind staff entice you to stay a little while longer. However, the food is what makes leaving so tough. Not only is it one of the few establishments in the city that understands what to do when you want a flat white instead of a cappuccino, but fresh fruit pastries, brioche cream rolls, and flaky croissants are made fresh every day on the premises. You'll be here for a long, so take off your outerwear and settle down.

Cucchi Pasta Shop

Pasticceria Cucchi is a bustling corner shop on Corso Genova. Its bright green awning and retro lettering challenge you to go by without taking a peek. This ancient café has been serving coffee and pastries since

1936, and it remains much the same as it did nearly a century ago. Small cakes and spherical panettones are surrounded by waiters in waistcoats and bow ties, while sophisticated older ladies with tiny dogs and even smaller handbags sit at the tables on the sidewalk outside. It's here that you may get a true taste of 1930s Milan. Prospective buyers are probably thumbing through a broadsheet rather than quickly perusing their likes and remarks.

Gogol and Company

Save Gogol & Company as a bookmark for a side of independent reading to go with your coffee. This place, which combines a bookstore, café, and exhibition area, offers something different every time you visit. Huge leather couches invite you to cozy up with whatever book you've chosen off the shelf, which is probably a book by an obscure author or a boutique publishing outfit. In addition to offering a wide range of organic drinks and pastries, they host jazz performances and organic wine tastings in the summer to liven up the piazza.

NIGHTLIFE AND BARS

Milan is considered to have one of the best nightlife scenes in Europe, partly because of its high proportion of young professionals. Locals take their celebrations very seriously, whether it's in divey pubs, clubs, or discos. In addition to being the center of fashion and culture in Italy, the city is also the greatest spot for "aperitivos" in the country. Aperitivo, the happy hour tradition of one or two drinks and some delicious canapés, may have originated in the city, but it was undoubtedly refined here and is a mainstay of Milan's nightlife.

Milan's Top Nightlife Districts

Brera for a lavish evening out. Adorable pedestrian cafes and wine bars in this area north of the La Scala opera building draw a pretty polished crowd despite its bohemian, shabby-chic aspect.

Locals' bohemian get-together: Navigli. Even though visitors only go as far as Navigli, this eccentric neighborhood surrounded by two old canals is brimming with trendy pubs and clubs that residents generally attend.

Enjoy drinks and breathtaking views in Piazza del Duomo. In Piazza del Duomo, elegant eateries and bars line the walkways as visitors and naive locals take in the views of the Duomo, Galleria Vittorio Emanuele II, and other sites.

Corso Como for disco dancing and velvet ropes. Save your energy for trying to enter any of the posh dance clubs around Garibaldi station on Corso Como and the side streets unless you're willing to pay the doorman 20 euros to be added to the list and are dressed to impress.

Corso Como for disco dancing and velvet ropes. Save your energy for trying to enter any of the posh dance clubs around Garibaldi station on Corso Como and the side streets unless you're willing to pay the doorman 20 euros to be added to the list and are dressed to impress.

Cocktail Bars

Mag Cafè: A landmark in Navigli, offering superb aperitivo appetizers, a vintage vibe, and well-crafted drinks.

Radetzky: This well-known Milanese pub is kid-friendly and has a great aperitivo hour. The hand-cut potato chips are sure to please little ones.

Dry Milano: While pizza is usually enjoyed with beer or wine, Dry Milano serves pizza and drinks in a classy atmosphere, and it works! close to the hotel-heavy Central Station and Porta Nuova districts.

GinO12: Milan's first gin bar has plenty of things to love, including its industrial-chic Navigli location, a vast gin selection, and unique creations.

Dolce & Gabbana Bar Martini: Located on chic Corso Venezia, this sensual bar offers breakfast, aperitivo, and dinners inspired by Sicily and is every bit as glamorous as a Dolce & Gabbana gown.

Rita & drinks: Known for its custom drinks and warm, casual atmosphere, this Navigli landmark is highly regarded.

N'Ombra de Vin: Known for its enormous wine cellar that boasts the best collection in Milan, N'Ombra de Vin serves up delicious antipasto platters that include cheese and salumi.

Nottingham Forest: This Porta Monforte hangout is worth the journey because of its quirky, unique décor and very inventively prepared and presented drinks.

ATTRACTIONS AND SIGHTSEEING

THE DUOMO

Cost and Operating Hours

Free to access; permissions are needed in certain regions every day from 9 a.m. to 7 p.m.

Advice: Explore the department store La Rinascente, located near Piazza del Duomo. La Rinascente Rooftop is a food hall with three eating options, including a laid-back bar and café with breathtaking views of the Duomo, located on the seventh story!

The Duomo ought to be your first stop in Milan if you only have time to see one thing. Taking over 500 years to build, Milan's Duomo is regarded as the biggest and most distinctive Gothic structure in all of Italy. It's also easy to see why the Duomo is regarded as a masterpiece after spending some time there. Thousands, no, precisely 2,300 finely carved sculptures adorn the outside, illustrating biblical tales and religious personalities alike, including the crucifixion of Jesus. Its interior design is significantly more elaborate. There are a thousand more sculptures inside, along with enormous marble columns, ornate ceilings, eye-catching stained-glass windows, and an abundance of artwork scattered throughout. The attention to detail also extends to the flooring, which is covered in marble with geometric patterns.

Another characteristic that sets the Duomo apart is its easily accessible roof. Travelers may enjoy views of the plaza below as well as up-close observations of the Duomo's intricate buttresses, pinnacles, and spires from this location. Don't forget to get a glimpse of the Madonna, situated atop the tallest tower. The church covered the golden monument during World War II so it wouldn't be easily seen from planes during the conflict.

Witnessing the majesty of this chapel is said to be worth the long lines and swarms of people that come to see it. Reviewers claim that you have to see the whole cathedral—inside and out—as well as the peak to appreciate its magnificence. Some recommended downloading an audio tour when visiting the Duomo to have a deeper understanding of its intricate history. There are also guided tours available, many of which include a visit to The Last Supper. It's better to schedule an early morning visit to avoid sharing the area with throngs of tourists, which you will undoubtedly encounter.

Tickets for Duomo

The Duomo is located in the heart of the city, just outside the Duomo metro station. Although there are small costs to visit certain portions of the church, admission is free. It costs 8 euros (about $9) for adults to enter the Duomo and 4 euros (around $4.50) for children aged 6 to 18. Expect to spend at least 16 euros (about $18) per adult for a ticket that allows access to the roof; the cost of the ticket varies depending on whether you want to use the elevator or the steps to get to the terrace.

Daily hours for the Duomo are 9 a.m. to 7 p.m. (the last entrance is at 6 p.m.). The church's roof, crypt, on-site museum, and other points of interest have their hours.

SFORZA CASTLE

Cost and Operating Hours

Free admission to the castle; 5 euros, or around $5.50, to the museum

The castle is open every day from 7 a.m. to 7:30 p.m.

Open Tuesday through Sunday from 10 a.m. to 5:30 p.m.

Advice: The Oh Bej! Oh, Bej! Christmas celebration at Piazza Castello will enchant you if you're traveling to Milan in the first part of December. The four-day fair features artisan goods and regional specialties to celebrate the feast of Sant'Ambrogio, Milan's patron saint.

Some of the best cultural organizations in the city are housed on the property of this historic fortress, which served as the palace of Milan's most powerful kings. It's also among the best strongholds in Europe. Less than a mile northwest of the Duomo, Castello Sforzesco is a landmark of Milan and home to several art and history-focused museums and galleries. The Pinacoteca, also known as the Picture Gallery, the Museo delle Arti Decorative, the Museum of Decorative Arts, the Museo

Egizio, the Egyptian Museum, and many more are available. One of the biggest collections of musical instruments in all of Europe may be found in the Museo Degli Strumenti Musicali. Considering all of the institutions on site, many people think the entry fee is rather reasonable. Travelers recommend seeing the Pietà Rondanini, Michelangelo's last masterwork, at the Museo della Pietà Rondanini if you're short on time.

Travelers believe the Castello Sforzesco is worth a trip even if you don't have time to see any museums or exhibits because of the beautiful architecture and lush gardens. The Parco Sempione, which has pedestrian pathways, a small reservoir, cafés, and its points of interest, is linked to the Castello Sforzesco.

You may visit the castle for free, but if you want to go to any of the museums, entry is 5 euros (about $5.50) for adults and 3 euros (roughly $3.50) for young people (ages 18 to 25); children and adolescents under the age of 17 are admitted free of charge. For an extra 5 euros, you may hire audio commentary in English at the on-site bookshop. This could be particularly helpful since some recent visitors reported that there wasn't much information in English in the museums. The institutions welcome guests Tuesday through Sunday from 10 a.m. to 5:30 p.m. The citadel is open every day from 7 a.m. to 7:30 p.m. Saturdays at 11 a.m. are when the institutions provide guided tours in English. The Cadorna FN, Lanza, and Cairoli Castello metro stations are within a short distance from the Castello Sforzesco.

GALLERIA VITTORIO EMANUELE II

The stunning interiors of this lavish shopping complex make it worth a visit even if you are unable to make any purchases there. Designed at the height of the 19th-century belle époque, this Galleria is a sumptuous shopping complex with an arcade made of steel and glass that houses high-end Italian labels like Prada, Gucci, and Armani. Fun fact: The first Prada shop, which opened its doors in 1913, was located here. The original register is even on display! There are other places to buy, such as boutiques selling designer clothing and bookshops filled with trendy magazines. Additionally, there are a few cafés and eateries within.

Travelers agree that the mall's grand architecture, eye-catching murals, and elaborate floor tiling are well worth a quick stop, regardless of price. Recent visitors indeed advise that you should expect large crowds.

The Galleria, which links the Piazza della Scala with the Piazza del Duomo, is located off the Duomo metro station. Go to the center octagon of the structure and "step on the bull" before you leave. It's said that if you turn your heel three times on a bull mosaic on the Galleria floor, good things will come your way. While the galleria is always open and free to enter, each shop has its hours.

FINAL SUPPER

Santa Maria delle Grazie Plaza, 2

Cost and Operating Hours

Adults pay 15 euros ($16.50); children under the age of 17 go free.

Tuesday–Sun 8:15 a.m.–7 p.m.

The famous "The Last Supper" (also known as "Il Cenacolo") by Leonardo da Vinci, dating from the fifteenth century, is housed within the Santa Maria delle Grazie cathedral in Milan. The artwork, which depicts the moment when Christ informs his apostles that one of them would betray him, is very moving, particularly in light of the events it has endured, such as a bombing during World War II and a flood. Despite having been repaired in the past, the picture still deteriorates due to the drywall painting method used by da Vinci.

Travelers still go to Santa Maria to see the picture in person because of its splendor, despite its state. Furthermore, subsequent visitors have said that the artwork is a masterpiece. Reviewers have said that seeing "The Last Supper" in person was breathtaking and urged visitors to examine it more closely since it is rich in detail (each apostle at the table has a unique expression). Some even said that as they stood in front of the picture, they started to become upset. While the mural is undoubtedly the main draw, visitors are also advised spending some time exploring the area. Apart from the artwork, Santa Maria's immaculate Renaissance building contributed to the church's designation as a UNESCO World Heritage Site. The only grievance expressed by guests? Due to crowds, you are only allowed to examine the artwork for 15 minutes before being escorted away.

Tips for watching "The Last Supper"

Tuesday through Sunday, from 8:15 a.m. to 7 p.m., is when you may see the artwork. Remember: Reservations must be made in advance. It is recommended that you make reservations several weeks, if not a month, in advance of your visit due to its popularity (you may make reservations up to three months in advance). Tickets are available at Viva Tickets. Adults 25 years of age and above pay 15 euros (about $16.50) for tickets, while adults 24 to 18 years old pay 12 euros (around

$13). Those under the age of seventeen are admitted free of charge. The first Sunday of each month provides free admission to the museum; online reservations are still required. Even if your preferred time and date aren't available on your first try, reviewers suggest checking the ticket website again later.

Once your fifteen minutes are over, you'll exit and go to the Cenacolo Vinciano Museum, which has pictures and information on all the repairs made to the painting. Additionally, there is a little outside patio where guests may see the spire of the church.

Directions to "The Last Supper"

Conciliazione and Cadorna FN are the nearest metro stations; tram 16 stops nearby as well.

SHOPPING AND FASHION

FASHION DISTRICT: QUADRILATERO d'ORO

Is the shopping district for fashion and shopping.

The Fashion Quadrilateral, or Quadrilatero della Moda in Milan, is one of the most well-known luxury shopping locations in the world. The neighborhood is named after the four affluent avenues that cross it: Corso Venezia, Manzoni, Della Spiga, and Montenapoleone. Borgospesso, Santo Spirito, Gesù, Sant'Andrea, and Bagutta are some more lovely streets.

Following the yearly study "Main Streets Across the World," the Fashion Quadrilateral consistently ranks among the most significant retail avenues in the world, along with Fifth Avenue in New York and Avenue des Champs Elysees in Paris. The renowned Via Montenapoleone came in second place on the podium in 2023.

Global shoppers visit the showrooms and boutiques to peruse, shop, and take in the excellent design and taste of the shops, which are consistently the height of elegance.

If you get yourself there, go to the "Piazza del Quadrilatero," which connects Via Sant'Andrea and Corso Venezia. After 500 years as a private location, the Archbishop's Seminary is finally accessible to the general public.

Both the building and its large central courtyard have undergone extensive renovations. Upmarket hotels, major fashion companies, and a boutique featuring cult streetwear brands are housed inside the sixteenth-century colonnade.

Take in the views as you stroll about the courtyard, stop by one of the upscale eateries tucked away among the shops, engage in some activities, or just discover one of Milan's once-secret locales that is now open to the public.

Luxurious shopping and Italian culture can be found in Milan's Fashion District, which also has some neighboring museums where you can learn about the history of the city. Additional options include the well-known Museo Bagatti Valsecchi home museum, the product of an incredible late nineteenth-century collection tale, and the museum of clothing, fashion, and image at Palazzo Morando.

Discover shopping, elegance, style, and culture at every stunning turn in this central Milan neighborhood.

OUTLET MALLS

Outlet boutiques in Milan provide the peak of Italian haute couture at prices up to 70% lower than suggested retail. You may find all of the big-name brands as well as non-clothing items like accessories, home décor, electronics, and cosmetics at these stores, which are spread around the city. Some of the best are massive shopping malls with a variety of food choices, entertainment options, and discount shops where you can shop till you drop.

Serravalle's Designer Outlet

Designer Outlet Serravalle is more than just a premium fashion outlet; it's also a picturesque shopping hamlet with town squares, fountains, strollable roads, and restaurants and bars. One of Europe's most well-known shopping destinations, it is about an hour's drive from Milan and boasts hundreds of boutique boutiques spread over 37,000 square meters.

During your shopping spree, you may come across the latest fashions from Armani, Burberry, Bvlgari, Fendi, Dolce & Gabbana, Gucci, Prada, Versace, and many more companies. All year, discounts range from 30% to 70% off. In addition to clothing, you could find accessories, cosmetics, home décor, and other items. The town also contains a children's play area.

Address: 1 Via della Moda, Serravalle Scrivia AL 15069, Italy.

Every day, starting at 10 a.m. to 8 p.m.

Vicolungo's Fashion Stores

Vicolungo The Style Outlets, with 147 unique enterprises, is part of a cheap outlet network that draws over 4 million visitors each year. You may find a broad variety of brands here, from Armani and Pollini to Nike and Levi's. A broad selection of jewelers, shoe stores, accessory shops, GAP, Under Armour, and even watchmakers are offering reductions of up to 70% off the usual price.

The Hamlet has restaurants, cafés, two kid-friendly playgrounds with carousels and climbing towers, and even a children's museum. The A4 freeway links Milan with Turin, taking around 50 minutes.

Address: 1 Piazza Santa Caterina, Vicolungo NO. 28060, Italy.

Open from 10 a.m. to 8 p.m. every Monday through Thursday from 10 a.m. to 9 p.m. On Friday and Sunday.

Village Franciacorta Outlet

With around 190 shops and services, Franciacorta Outlet Hamlet is a unique and popular fashion outlet intended to mimic a little hamlet with covered and open areas. International brands accessible include Under Armour, Nike, L'Oréal, Adidas, Guess, Boggi Milano, Tru Trussardi, Plein Sport, and Pollini. They are all up to 70% off their retail price. Dining options include bars, sit-down restaurants, and fast meals such as McDonald's. With all of your fashion needs satisfied in one place, it's easy to spend the day browsing the many options.

This Lake Garda center is around an hour's drive from Milan. Even better, shuttle bus providers offer retail discounts in addition to round-trip transportation.

The site location is 1/2 Piazza Cascina Moie, 25050 Rodengo Saiano BS, Italy.

Every day, starting at 10 a.m. to 8 p.m.

Tel: (39) 030-681-0364

Scalo Milano Outlet.

Scalo Milano Outlet & More is one of the closest outlet malls to Milan's downtown, with more than 150 businesses and services. It is designed to mimic a retail town and is built on top of a converted industrial complex, as are many other stores. Converse, Ferrari, Diadora, Jack & Jones, Napapijri, Kappa, New Balance, Pepe Jeans, Reebok, Puma, Swarovski, The North Face, and Alessi are just a few of the global brands represented here. There are discounts ranging from 30 to 70%.

This shop favors casual things above couture. A children's area, a hair salon, and even a tailor are provided as supplementary services. It is located around 9 kilometers from the city center.

Location: 8, Via Milano, Triulzi, MI, 20085, Italy.

Open from 10am till nine p.m. Every day

Phone: (904) 947-0350.

LOCAL MARKETS

The Via Fauchè market is a low-cost and historically important shopping destination for apparel and accessories. If you want to avoid crowds, Tuesdays are the ideal day to go; however, Saturdays, when there are more booths, provide more alternatives.

The best Made-in-Italy brands are on display alongside bigger names and smaller ones. If you want to buy clothes, shoes, or cashmere sweaters, go to the kiosks at Piazza Caneva. If you want to purchase designer footwear, go to Piazza Gerusalemme.

Tuesdays, 8:30 a.m. to 1 p.m.; Saturdays, 8:30 a.m. to 5

Check out the Viale Papiniano Market for bargains.

This is the Viale Papiniano market, with a kilometer of stalls, many of which sell designer fashion goods. You've come to the right place whether you're searching for athletic or conventional shoes, baggage, and much more. Keep an eye out for the "Deadstock" label, which indicates new, unsold stuff from retailers and outlets that is just as good a bargain as the unlabeled product.

While you're at it, replenish your pantry with fresh fish, meat, and vegetables. Go in the early morning.

Tuesdays, 7:30 a.m. - 2 p.m. 7.30 a.m. On Saturdays. - 6pm

The market's exclusivity in Via San Marco

It is strongly advised that you travel through the shopping alleys of Milan's old center, which are framed by the gorgeous structures of the Via San Marco Market, better known as the Brera Market. In comparison to other street markets, the prices are higher, but the quality is superior.

On Thursday, look for La Marucca, one of the vendors selling beautiful cashmere and knitwear from Forte dei Marmi. Look through the leather bag and glove booths in this large outdoor shop; everything is quite elegant and unique.

7.30 a.m. on Monday and Thursday. - 2 p.m.

Fiera di Sinigaglia: History on display.

The Fiera di Sinigaglia, located in Milan's fascinating Navigli area, is the city's oldest flea market, dating back to the nineteenth century. It provides a true look into the city's history.

Vintage apparel and accessories may be blended with vinyl recordings, oriental trinkets, and a wide variety of other objects. Are they also the greatest? Evening dresses with semi-precious stone necklaces and jewelry are ideal for a theme party or a wild night on the town. It'll be like browsing through ancient royal clothing. Saturdays at 8 a.m. - 6 p.m.

ARTS AND CULTURE

MUSEUMS

Milan's museums house thousands of years of artwork, culture, history, antiques, and exhibits on topics ranging from current art and Renaissance painters to natural history and industrial development. Milan is a European art hotspot, with galleries across the city showing unique works in a variety of media such as sculptures, paintings, drawings, and photography. But it is much more than just a collection of paintings. Milan also has a huge number of special-interest museums covering topics such as Leonardo da Vinci, fashion design, and modern Italian history.

This is the place to go if you are interested in history, art, or culture. Grab a Tourist Museum Card to save money when visiting some of Milan's greatest museums.

Castello Sforzesco

Sforzesco Castle, an iconic depiction of Milan, is a museum built in a medieval castle that explores a wide variety of bizarre historical subjects. The museum has a section dedicated to furniture. There's another area with an art gallery. The third room has a collection of musical instruments, while the fourth houses one of the country's largest collections of Renaissance statues and sculptures. The Rondanini Pietà, Michelangelo's last work, is included in one of the most outstanding collections.

The museum has 10 collections; select your favorite and then explore the others. It's located in the center of the city.

Location: 20121 Milano MI, Italy; Piazza Castello

Open every day at 7:30 a.m. to 7:30 p.m.

Brera Pinacoteca

Pinacoteca di Brera, one of Milan's greatest art galleries, is a popular cultural center. It has one of Italy's largest art collections, including works by renowned Italian artists such as Caravaggio, Mantegna, Raphael, and others. The highlights of the museum include Tintoretto's "Discovery of the Body of Saint Mark," Hayez's "The Kiss," Mantegna's "The Lamentation of Christ," Caravaggio's "Supper at Emmaus," and Raphael's "The Marriage of the Virgin."

The Orto Botanico di Brera, a beautiful botanical garden, sits right beyond the museum. It is a refuge where you may relax and reflect on what you have witnessed.

Address: 28 Via Brera, Milano, MI 20121 Italy.

Leonardo da Vinci National Museum of Science and Technology.

The National Museum of Science and Technology Leonardo da Vinci (Museo Nazionale della Scienza e della Tecnologia Leonardo da Vinci) has hundreds of interactive exhibits that illustrate the history of scientific progress. This friendly museum celebrating Leonardo da Vinci is primarily dedicated to his works and achievements, but it also has an extensive collection of tools, automobiles, trains, and aircraft, as well as reproductions of Da Vinci's concepts and an investigation of whether or not they were possible.

It also has interactive labs where adults and children may undertake STEM activities related to energy, biotechnology, and other current themes. It is located in the Sant'Ambrogio area in the city center and is housed in a beautiful 16th-century monastery.

Address: 21 San Vittore Street, Milan, MI 20123.

Available: Tuesday through Friday, 10 a.m. to 6 p.m.; Saturday and Sunday, 10 a.m. to 7 p.m. (Closed on Mondays).

The Milanese Palazzo Reale or Royal Palace

The Royal Palace (Palazzo Reale Milano) has exhibitions on the many Spanish, French, and other rulers who contributed to the country's development, highlighting Italy's tangled and shattered past. It analyzes the dynasties of the Visconti, Sforza, and Habsburgs, among others, who have ruled over this peninsula in the past, demonstrating how Italy evolved from a center of culture and empire to a hotly disputed territory to the nation it is now.

You will be able to study about emperors, kings, fascists, and the present democratic republic. This unique museum in the city center has artifacts, memorabilia, artwork, and other things that eloquently reflect this rich history.

Location: 12 Piazza del Duomo, Milano, MI, 20122.

Open Tuesday through Wednesday at 10 a.m. to 7.30 p.m. on Fridays through Sundays, at 10 a.m. to 10.30 p.m. on Thursdays (closed Mondays).

Milan's Museum of Cultural Arts (Mudec)

The Museum of Cultures, often known as Mudec (Museo delle Culture di Milano), is a contemporary art museum with worldwide anthropological exhibits. The museum, designed by renowned architect David Chipperfield, transformed an old industrial structure into an eye-catching modern institution and was inaugurated in 2015. The museum hosts some excellent temporary, rotating, and visiting exhibits that span a broad variety of subjects, including Chinese immigration, ancient Egypt, and modern and contemporary artists. It has shown works by renowned artists like Frida Kahlo, Roy Lichtenstein, and Wassily Kandinsky.

The museum hosts lectures, seminars, guest speakers, and an event space, so there is always something going on there. It takes around 20 minutes to go southwest of the city center.

Address: 56 Via Tortona, MI 20144 Milan, Italy.

THEATERS AND MUSIC VENUES

Milan has several fantastic live music venues. Given Milan's reputation for creating internationally recognized fashion, it's no surprise that the city boasts an equally sophisticated music scene.

Milano Blue Note

Milan's renowned Blue Note showcases some of the best live jazz, soul, Latin, and R&B acts in the vicinity. The Blue Note brand, which has sites in New York, Tokyo, Sao Paolo, and other cities, has been intimately identified with jazz since its inception in 1981.

The jazz club is also well-known for its superb cuisine and beverages. Tables and chairs surround the stage area, making it easy for guests to enjoy food, beverages, and live music all at the same time. Even though it seems to be an upscale establishment, everyone is made to feel welcome with kind, courteous treatment.

Address: 37 Via Pietro Borsieri, Milan, Italy 20159.

Theatre Nidaba

Milan's Nidaba Theatre is a prominent live music venue that hosts a variety of bands and performers. Nidaba's versatile schedule includes rock, soul, funk, blues, jazz, and more. It is known for showcasing the greatest local musicians with regular guest appearances by international artists.

The relaxed ambience and courteous personnel of this popular restaurant ensure that the customer is as diverse as the musical choices, attracting people of all ages and socioeconomic backgrounds. Because of its tiny size and old style, the venue radiates a rustic atmosphere that is ideal for any kind of event.

Location: Milan, Italy; Via Emilio Gola 12, 20143.

City of Social Music

Social Music City is a large music arena in Milan designed to showcase cutting-edge sounds during festivals. The event venue draws bands and performers from a variety of musical genres, including rock, electronica, and almost everything in between, and often hosts international concerts.

Social Music City, housed in a spacious and futuristic hangar, has cutting-edge lighting and sound equipment, making it one of the city's most sophisticated performance spaces. On-site eating and bars are available, and when the right bands come through town, the venue's massive size allows for some fairly crazy celebrations.

Address: 3A, Giovanni Lorenzini Via, Milano, Italy 20139.

Biko Group

The sensuous Biko Club in Milan serves up a seductive blend of hip-hop, R&B, and soul music. The casual music hall, which showcases a mix of present and retrospective acts, is well-known for hosting some of Milan's most lively parties.

There is a separate chillout zone for people who prefer to converse rather than dance, and the modest drink menu complements the environment. The facility is named after the South African anti-apartheid icon Steve Biko and its noble objective is to cultivate unity and diversity in the city.

Address: 40 Via Ettore Ponti, Milano, Italy 20143.

PARKS AND RECREATION

SEMPIONE PARK

Parco Sempione refers to the vast green space around Castello Sforzesco. From 1890 to 1893, the English landscape park was established.

The park covers more than 47 hectares. It includes a beautiful man-made lake that attracts a variety of birds, as well as trees, bushes, and flowers sprinkled throughout its brilliant green lawns.

The construction of the park

Hundreds of animals, plants, and beautiful constructions live in the green space. It is worth seeing the following structures:

The Milan Triennale is an event that celebrates Italian avant-garde architecture and fine art.

The Civic Aquarium was built for the 1906 Expo and is situated in Milan. More than 100 distinct species are kept in the 36 tanks.

Arena Civica: Built-in 1806 with Napoleon present, the Arena Civica is a spectacular amphitheater that accommodates concerts and other events.

Arco della Pace: The triumphal arch was built in 1807 to commemorate Napoleon's victories, but when the Austrian Empire took over Milan, it was halted for a brief time. It was completed in 1838, coinciding with Italy's unification.

Central and beautiful.

When the weather is beautiful, both tourists and inhabitants gather in Milan's major park, Parco Sempione, which boasts large green spaces for relaxing. Because the trees mostly offer shade in the groomed areas, the park does not provide as much shade as one would want during the summer.

Whereabouts

Accompanying Castello Sforcesco.

Timetable

Daily hours are 6:30 a.m. to 9:00 p.m.

Move about.

Metro lines: M1 in Cadorna, M1 in Cairoli, and M2 in Lanza.

Transportation: Lines 1, 2, 4, 12, 14, and 19.

Lines 18, 50, 37, 58, 61, and 94 are bus routes.

Nearby Locations

Triennale: 190 meters.

Sforzesco Castello (472 meters)

Leonardo da Vinci's The Last Supper (898 meters)

Archaeological Museum of Milan (903 meters)

San Maurizio at the Maggiore Monastery (910 meters)

NAVIGLI CANALS

The Navigli, one of Milan's most charming and appealing areas, is well-known for its canal-side cafés and bars, wonderfully crafted bridges, galleries, and trendy concept stores. The streets that surround the Naviglio Grande and Naviglio Pavese are known as the "Navigli," and they give insight into how the city transported products centuries ago. Is it true that Milan and Switzerland were formerly connected by the Naviglio Grande? These canals contributed to Milan's growth and prosperity via trade. Admirers of architecture will notice that the banks of the Navigli are home to antique wash house structures with wooden beam roofs known as case di ringhiera, as well as dwellings constructed around a central courtyard.

Tourists like visiting the antique market held on the last Sunday of the month, as well as the artisan shops in the Navigli. Because of their closeness, it is advised that you visit both Darsena and Navigli. Boat trips are an enjoyable way to explore the region. But be warned: if you are allergic to bugs, summers in the Navigli will be quite unpleasant. Bicyclists like the Naviglio Martesana because it is possible to go 20 kilometers along the canal to reach the river Adda.

Even at night, the busy Navigli neighborhood in the center of Milan is a sight to see. The Porta Genova metro station, situated about a ten-minute walk west of the area, makes it easily accessible.

PUBLIC GARDENS

Milan has numerous large, beautiful parks where people may enjoy long walks or runs. Among the most well-known are Parco Sempione, the 640-hectare Parco Nord, and BAM, the Library of Trees, situated at the foot of the Bosco Verticale. Many smaller-scale gardens entice people with their natural elegance.

Gardens of Porta Venezia

Indro Montanelli Gardens are located in Milan's bright rainbow neighborhood.

It is a popular outdoor meeting location for young people and artists and is near to the GAM - Modern Art Gallery and the PAC - Contemporary Art Pavilion.

It's also an excellent place to spend a family day exploring the park's playground rides, planetarium, and Natural History Museum.

Or maybe to take a vacation from the fashion industry by shopping nearby, walking through the streets lined with thick trees, and breathing the fresh air.

To reach there, use the Palestro station and then the M1 underground (red line).

The Library of Trees, or Biblioteca degli Alberi (BAM)

A large open area is located at the foot of the Bosco Verticale, connecting Piazza Gae Aulenti to the Isola district.

The park is also wheelchair accessible, and the Catella Foundation organizes a variety of public activities such as children's games, outdoor gym equipment, and picnic spots. We encourage going by to see the diverse range of botanical species and areas that residents enjoy during their summer lunch breaks.

Getting there: M5 (lilac) Garibaldi or Isola stations, and subterranean M2 (green) Garibaldi or Gioia stops.

Portello's Alfa Romeo Industrial Park

This park, located between Viale Certosa and QT8, west of the city center in the Portello neighborhood, is a good example of urban renewal.

Admired for its incredibly long bench where guests can stop and take in the perfectly circular lake, perhaps after navigating the double helix spiral hill, this area is enjoyable to explore by meandering through the hedges and evenly spaced tree rows to learn about the astronomy-themed installations and sculptures.

Directions: Take the M5 (lilac) Metro line to Portello station.

DAY TRIPS FROM MILAN

LAKE COMO

Taking a day excursion from Milan to Lake Como provides a refreshing retreat into a world of spectacular natural beauty, elegant homes, and tiny villages. Located in the Lombardy region, just a short train ride north of Milan, Lake Como is known for its breathtaking landscapes, set against the backdrop of the Alps.

Getting There:

The journey begins with a convenient train ride from Milan's central station, Milano Centrale, to the town of Como, situated at the southern tip of the lake. The trip typically lasts about an hour, making it an easy and scenic route for travelers. Upon arrival in Como, visitors are greeted with the serene beauty of the lake, surrounded by mountains and dotted with elegant, pastel-coloured buildings.

Exploring Como:

In Como Town, you can start your adventure by exploring the charming streets, filled with cafes, boutiques, and historical sites. The Como Cathedral

(Duomo di Como) is a must-visit, with its outstanding Gothic and Renaissance architecture. For panoramic views of the lake and surrounding area, take the funicular railway up to the hilltop village of Brunate.

Lake Como via Boat:

To truly experience the beauty of Lake Como, take a boat tour from Como. The public ferries are a budget-friendly option to hop between lakeside towns, while private boat tours offer a more intimate and customizable experience. Highlights include the picturesque town of Bellagio, known as the "Pearl of the Lake," and Varenna, with its colorful waterfront and Villa Monastero's beautiful gardens.

Bellagio and Varenna:

Bellagio sits at the junction of the lake's two southern branches, offering spectacular views, luxurious villas, and lush gardens. Varenna, on the other hand, is quieter and exudes a more traditional charm with its narrow alleyways and waterfront promenade. Both towns are perfect for leisurely exploration, offering a glimpse into the luxurious lifestyle and historic elegance that Lake Como is famous for.

Local Cuisine:

No trip to Lake Como is complete without indulging in the local cuisine. Lakeside restaurants and cafes offer dishes featuring fresh fish from the lake, such as "Risotto con Filetti di Pesce Persico" (risotto with perch filets), paired with a glass of Lombardy wine. The region's Italian and Mediterranean influences ensure a delightful culinary experience.

Returning to Milan:

As the day winds down, head back to the Como train station for your return trip to Milan. The journey back offers a moment to reflect on the day's adventures and the serene beauty of Lake Como.

BERGAMO

A day trip from Milan to Bergamo offers a delightful escape into one of Lombardy's most picturesque cities. Just a short train ride away, Bergamo is divided into two distinct parts: the Città Alta (Upper City), a medieval hilltop town surrounded by Venetian walls, and the Città Bassa (Lower City), a vibrant, modern area. This guide will help you make the most of your day trip to Bergamo.

Morning: Departure and Arrival

Begin your adventure early by catching a train from Milan's Central Station to Bergamo. The journey takes approximately an hour, giving you a full day to explore. Upon arrival, head to the funicular railway for a scenic ride up to the Città Alta. The funicular not only offers great views but also conveniently connects you to the heart of Bergamo's historical center.

Exploring the Città Alta

Start your exploration of the Città Alta with a visit to the Piazza Vecchia, the heart of the old city. This square is surrounded by impressive buildings, including the

Palazzo della Ragione, the Campanone (bell tower), and the beautiful Biblioteca Angelo Mai. Climb the Campanone for panoramic views of the rooftops and the surrounding countryside.

Next, make your way to the Basilica di Santa Maria Maggiore, an architectural masterpiece with stunning interiors, including tapestries and inlaid marble floors. The adjoining Cappella Colleoni is a must-see for its remarkable Renaissance façade and interior artworks.

Lunch in the Old Town

By now, you'll have worked up an appetite. Bergamo's Città Alta offers numerous dining options where you can enjoy local specialties such as casoncelli (stuffed pasta) and polenta. Choose a restaurant to savor both the food and the surroundings.

Afternoon: More Exploration and Return to the Lower City

After lunch, stroll along the Venetian Walls (Mura Venete) that encircle the Città Alta, now a UNESCO World Heritage site. The walls offer more splendid views and a chance to walk off your lunch.

As the afternoon progresses, take the funicular back down to the Città Bassa. Here, you can admire the contrast between the medieval charm of the Città Alta and the vibrant, modern life of the lower city. Explore the Accademia Carrara, a renowned art gallery, or stroll through the Sentierone, the heart of the Città Bassa, lined with cafes and shops.

Evening: Return to Milan

Conclude your day trip with a leisurely return train ride to Milan, reflecting on the rich history and beautiful landscapes of Bergamo. Whether you're interested in art, history, or simply soaking up the atmosphere of a Lombard city, Bergamo offers a memorable day out that complements the urban buzz of Milan.

Tips for Your Trip

- Check train times in advance to maximize your day.

- Wear comfortable shoes for walking on cobblestone streets.

- Consider purchasing a Bergamo Card for discounts on transportation and attractions.

CINQUE TERRE

Cinque Terre, a UNESCO World Heritage site, is a collection of five ancient, colorful villages (Monterosso al Mare, Vernazza, Corniglia, Manarola, and Riomaggiore) perched along the rugged Ligurian coast.

Morning: Departure and Arrival

Your experience begins early with a train travel from Milan to La Spezia or straight to one of the Cinque Terre towns, depending on the available connections. The journey may take between 3 to 4 hours, so getting an early train is suggested to optimize your time in Cinque Terre. Upon arrival, obtain a Cinque Terre Card, which enables unlimited train travel between the towns and access to hiking trails and Wi-Fi.

Exploring the Villages

Begin your trip at Riomaggiore, the southernmost hamlet, noted for its ancient charm and stunning beach cliffs. Enjoy a leisurely walk through the village's small alleyways, leading up to a lovely vista of the Ligurian Sea.

Next, get on a train to Manarola, noted for its scenic port and colorful buildings. Manarola provides a superb chance for photography aficionados, particularly from the water's edge to look back at the town.

Continue to Corniglia, the only settlement not right by the sea, located on a peninsula. Reach there by ascending the Lardarina staircase, a set of stairs that give beautiful views along the way. Corniglia is calmer and more secluded, great for enjoying a more tranquil pace.

Vernazza, undoubtedly the most picturesque of the five villages, is your next destination. With its natural waterfront and vibrant main center, Vernazza is crowded with cafés and boutiques. Take a minute to relax by the waterfront and absorb the bright scene.

Conclude your village hopping at Monterosso al Mare, the biggest of the Cinque Terre settlements. Monterosso boasts stunning beaches, making it a great site for a refreshing swim or a sunbathing session on the Italian Riviera.

Lunch and Leisure

Choose one of the villages for lunch, where you may sample local delicacies like fresh fish, pesto (originating from this area), and Focaccia di Recco. Many restaurants provide terraces with sea views, providing for a picturesque eating experience.

Afternoon: Hiking and Beach Time

If time and energy permit, participate in a trekking adventure between several of the communities. The route from Vernazza to Monterosso is particularly famous for its spectacular views of the coastline and the Mediterranean vegetation. Remember, the Cinque Terre Card provides entry to these routes.

Alternatively, spend your afternoon lounging on the beaches of Monterosso, where you may unwind and reflect on the day's experiences.

Evening: Return to Milan

As the day closes down, drive back to La Spezia or straight from one of the villages to Milan. The return ride is a time to recover and think about the spectacular views and experiences of Cinque Terre.

TURIN

Turin, or Torino in Italian, is distinguished for its exquisite squares, world-class museums, and the landmark Mole Antonelliana. Here's how to make the most of your day trip to this magnificent city.

Morning: Departure and Arrival

Begin your day early by getting a train from Milan to Turin, with the travel lasting roughly 1 to 2 hours depending on the service you pick. Arriving in Turin, start your journey in the city center, where the enormous Piazza Castello serves as the appropriate starting point. This area is bordered by great structures such as the Palazzo Reale (Royal Palace) and Palazzo Madama.

Exploring the Royal Palace and Egyptian Museum

A visit to the Palazzo Reale, the old royal palace of the House of Savoy, gives an insight into the sumptuous lifestyle of Italy's royal past. The palace has a significant collection of art, furniture, and decorations. Just a short walk from the palace, you'll discover the Museo Egizio, the world's oldest museum devoted solely to Egyptian archaeology and ethnography. It offers a huge collection of relics, including mummies, papyri, and the Tomb of Kha.

Lunch at the City Center

For lunch, indulge in Piedmontese cuisine, famed for its rich tastes and high-quality ingredients. Try local favorites such as agnolotti del plin (little ravioli with a meat filling), vitello tonnato (thinly sliced veal in a creamy tuna sauce), and of course, the famed truffles when in season. Numerous restaurants and cafés in the city center provide these delicacies.

Afternoon: Visit the Mole Antonelliana and Stroll Along the Po River

After lunch, make your way to the Mole Antonelliana. Originally planned as a synagogue, this tall edifice is now home to the National Cinema Museum. The museum provides a trip through the history of film in a highly interactive manner. Take the panorama lift to the summit for stunning views of the city and the surrounding Alps.

Next, take a stroll along the banks of the Po River, which provides a calm getaway from the city bustle. The Parco del Valentino, situated along the river, is one of Turin's most attractive parks and features a wonderful model of a medieval town, the Borgo Medievale.

Evening: Return to Milan

Conclude your day with a return train to Milan. Turin's beautiful piazzas and cafés give an ideal environment to unwind and reflect on your day's experiences before returning.

FESTIVALS AND EVENTS

WEEKEND OF MILAN FASHION

Milan Fashion Week, also known as Settimana della moda di Milano in Italian, is a semi-annual fashion trade show that takes place in Milan, Italy. Future spring/summer clothing is shown in September/October of each year, while upcoming fall/winter clothing is shown in February/March. Numerous designers showcase their upcoming collections and fresh designs. Along with New York, Paris, London, and Tokyo, Milan Fashion Week is one of the "Big Five" global fashion weeks.

Milan Fashion Week's History

This fashion week is one of the "Big Four Fashion Weeks," as they are known. There has been a men's and women's fashion week at Milan Fashion Week every two years since 1958. The London, Paris, and New York fashion weeks are the other three.

The dates for Milan Fashion Week

Catwalk runways are created on Milan's cobblestone streets in September, February, January, and June. Trends of any kind that you could think of are being shown. The spring/summer fashion presentations for men and women happen in June and September, respectively. For women, the Fall/Winter exhibitions take place in February, and for men, in January.

Is an invitation required to attend Fashion Week?

It is dependent upon several factors. Some concerts need an invitation, even if there are outdoor events that are free to attend. However, you could get a peek at others. You may pre-register for an after-party, which guarantees a great time with other fashionistas, celebs, and designers if you are unable to attend the event you want to.

Where Are the Shows Held?

That might be said to happen in almost any place on Milan's cobblestone streets. Additionally, there are independent exhibits. There are standard showrooms and studios, but some fashion shows happen in outdoor landmarks and historic locations. The main square in Milan, Piazza Duomo, the 15th-century Castello Sforzesco courtyard, and Arco della Pace in Parco

Sempione are a few of the locations where the general public may see the fashion shows.

Which Well-Known Designers Will Milan Fashion Week Feature?

Fashion Week features displays by well-known designers and fashion brands. Among them are Armani, Jil Sander, Prada, Versace, John Richmond, Gucci, Missoni, Dolce & Gabbana, and Roberto Cavalli. Not only are large companies involved, but upcoming companies may also showcase their offerings. During Milan Fashion Week, Cristiano Burani, Stella Jean, Francesco Scognamiglio, Marco De Vincenzo, and Au jour le jour get the opportunity to present.

You are in for a great treat whether you have to attend fashion shows or you just want to stroll about and see what happens. Since it becomes crowded, you must make reservations for your accommodations in advance. Milan has a wonderful vitality. Months in advance of the events, all of the venue and concert information is available to see.

SALONE DEL MOBILE

One of the most important occasions in the design and furniture industries, the Salone del Mobile, sometimes called the Milan Furniture Fair, brings together professionals, designers, and enthusiasts from all over the world. This annual event, which takes place in Milan, Italy, showcases the most recent advancements in lighting, furniture, and other elements of interior design. In the design sector, it serves as a vibrant forum for the exchange of ideas, styles, and technological advancements.

Synopsis and Background

Founded in 1961 to increase Italian exports of furniture and furnishings, the Salone del Mobile has grown to become the largest trade show of its kind worldwide. The event is a component of the larger Milan Design Week, which also features the Fuorisalone, a collection of displays and events dispersed over several Milan neighborhoods.

What to Expect

The fair is held at the Fiera Milano complex in Rho and is divided into various sections: Classic, which draws on the values of tradition, craftsmanship and skill in the art of making furniture and objects; Design, which is devoted to the products that speak of functionality, innovation, and a great sense of style; and xLux, which is dedicated to timeless luxury reinterpreted in a contemporary vein.

Attendees may expect to witness a broad selection of items from high-end furniture to lighting solutions, outdoor furnishings, and office furniture, showing the current trends in living and workplaces. The event not only exhibits famous brands but also gives a platform for new designers and firms via the Salone Satellite, a segment devoted to under-35 designers.

Highlights & Features

- unique Exhibitions: Every edition of the Salone del Mobile showcases new designs, with pavilions packed with unique goods that defy traditional concepts of form, function, and beauty.

- International Focus: The event has a strong international component, with hundreds of exhibitors from across the globe and a considerable number of foreign guests, making it a truly global affair.

- lectures and Workshops: The expo offers a comprehensive program of lectures, workshops, and conversations hosted by famous designers, architects, and industry professionals, giving insights into current design trends and future directions.

- Networking chances: For professionals in the design and furniture sector, the Salone del Mobile provides unrivaled networking chances, allowing for the establishment of new business partnerships and collaborations.

ANNUAL EVENTS

Carnevale Ambrosiano (February) Carnival in Milan is celebrated later than in the rest of Italy: this delay is claimed to come from a plea given to the people by its patron saint, Ambrose, who could not make it back in time after a pilgrimage far from Milan. Colorful costumes flood the streets as bakeries fill with sweets such as tortellini and chiacchiere.

Milano Design Week (Mid-April) Commonly referred to as "Fuorisalone", this spontaneous celebration of design, art and culture has been held since the '80s outside the International Furniture Fair. Hundreds of events of all types plus the nice environment make it one of the greatest times to be in the city.

Fiori e sapori (Flowers and Flavours) sul Naviglio Grande (Mid-April) A display of florists and local producers that flood the area surrounding the canal with colors and delicious fragrances to welcome the coming of spring.

Milano Food Week (Early-MidMay) Since Milan hosted the World Expo in 2015, food has been a major element in the life of the city. Talks, show-cookings, tastings and other activities make the belly of the city come alive.

Arianteo (Summer) Fancy a movie but you don't want to be imprisoned in a theater throughout your stay? Every summer maxi-screens are put in some of the city's best locales, from parks to castles and ancient houses, for a three-month season of open-air events.

Villa Arconati Festival (July) Music fans will be delighted with this collection of Italian and worldwide musicians to be experienced in the gorgeous setting of an 18th-century palace, a tiny Versailles at the doorstep of Milan. Free shuttle buses leaving from the city center run on music days.

Milano Film Festival (September) This Festival brings together works from the worldwide independent scene, featuring screenings of rising artists and displaying a broad diversity of narratives and cultures.

Bookcity (Mid-November) For readers of all types, this event places the book at the middle of the stage with publishers, authors, readers and artists engaging in a weekend of lectures, conferences, presentations and workshops to promote reading and culture.

Artigiano in Fiera (First week of December) Loved by residents for its astounding selection of hand-crafted culinary products from all over the globe, this is virtually a necessary visit to choose some Christmas gifts while braving the throng.

PRACTICAL TIPS

SAFETY AND EMERGENCY INFORMATION

Public Hospitals and Clinics: Milan has many public hospitals equipped with emergency rooms (Pronto Soccorso) that give quick treatment. These hospitals provide a broad variety of services and are manned by personnel capable of managing different health conditions. Ospedale Maggiore Policlinico, Ospedale San Raffaele, and Ospedale Niguarda are among the notable hospitals in the city.

Private Hospitals and Clinics: For individuals who choose private healthcare, Milan boasts various private hospitals and clinics that provide high-quality treatments, sometimes with shorter waiting periods and more pleasant facilities. Private healthcare might be more costly, therefore it's important to get travel insurance that covers medical bills at private institutions.

Pharmacies: Pharmacies (Farmacie) are readily accessible throughout Milan and are the primary point of contact for minor illnesses and drug requirements. Many pharmacies provide 24-hour service, and you may distinguish them by the green cross sign. Pharmacists in Milan are often informed and may advise on minor health concerns and over-the-counter drugs.

Emergency Information

Emergency Numbers: For any health emergency, the number to phone is 112, which is the European Union's global emergency number. This number may be called from any phone, free of charge. It links callers to the proper emergency service, including medical crises, fire, and police.

Non-Emergency Medical Advice: For non-urgent medical advice, you may call the Guardia Medica, which offers medical aid during evenings, weekends, and holidays when conventional physicians' offices are closed. The service may assist over the phone or arrange home visits if required.

Ambulance Services: In case of a medical emergency requiring an ambulance, phoning 112 will guarantee that medical aid is delivered swiftly. Ambulance services in Milan are well-equipped to offer urgent treatment and transfer to the closest competent hospital.

Health Insurance and EHIC

Visitors from the European Union should have the European Health Insurance Card (EHIC), which permits access to the public healthcare system under the same conditions as Italian natives. Travelers from outside the EU are highly urged to acquire comprehensive travel health insurance to cover any medical costs incurred during their stay.

General Safety Tips

- Keep a list of emergency contacts on your person, including the location and phone number of your country's embassy or consulate in Milan.

- Be conscious of your health issues and bring required prescriptions with you, along with a doctor's letter detailing their usage, particularly if you're carrying prescription pharmaceuticals.

- Stay hydrated and protected from the sun during the warmer months, and be careful of your physical limitations when visiting the city.

ESSENTIAL ITALIAN PHRASES

Greetings and Basic Politeness

- Buongiorno (bwon-JOR-no) - Good morning
- Buonasera (bwon-ah-SEH-rah) - Good evening
- Buonanotte (bwon-ah-NOT-teh) - Good night
- Ciao (chow) - Hi/Bye (informal)
- Arrivederci (ah-ree-veh-DER-chee) - Goodbye (formal)
- Per favore (per fah-VOH-reh) - Please
- Grazie (GRAH-tsee-eh) - Thank you
- Grazie mille (GRAH-tsee-eh MEEL-leh) - Thank you very much
- Prego (PREH-goh) - You're welcome
- Scusa (SKOO-sah) - Excuse me (informal)
- Scusi (SKOO-zee) - Excuse me (formal)

Directions and Transportation

- Dove è la stazione? (DOH-veh eh lah stah-TSYOH-neh?) - Where is the station?
- Quanto dista il Duomo? (KWAN-toh DEE-stah eel DWOH-moh?) - How far is the Duomo?

- Un biglietto per il centro, per favore. (Oon bee-LYET-toh per eel CHEN-troh, per fah-VOH-reh) - A ticket to the center, please.

- Questo autobus va in centro? (KWEH-stoh ow-toh-BOOS vah in CHEN-troh?) - Does this bus go to the center?

- Dove posso trovare un taxi? (DOH-veh POHS-soh troh-VAH-reh on TAHK-see?) - Where can I find a taxi?

Dining and Food

- Un tavolo per due, per favore. (Oon TAH-voh-loh per DOO-eh, per fah-VOH-reh) - A table for two, please.

- Il menù, per favore. (eel meh-NOO, per fah-VOH-reh) - The menu, please.

- Cosa ci consiglia? (KOH-sah chee kohn-SEE-lyah?) - What do you recommend?

- Posso avere il conto? (POHS-soh ah-VEH-reh eel KON-toh?) - Can I have the bill?

- Sono allergico/a a... (SOH-noh ahl-LEHR-gee-koh/kah ah...) - I'm allergic to...

Shopping

- Quanto costa? (KWAN-toh KOH-stah?) - How much is it?

- Posso pagare con la carta? (POHS-soh pah-GAH-reh kohn lah KAR-tah?) - Can I pay with a card?

- Dove posso comprare...? (DOH-veh POHS-soh kom-PRAH-reh...?) - Where can I buy...?

- Posso provare questo? (POHS-soh proh-VAH-reh KWEH-stoh?) - Can I try this on?

Emergency and Health

- Aiuto! (ah-YOO-toh) - Help!

- Chiamo la polizia. (kee-AH-moh lah poh-LEE-tsee-ah) - I'm calling the police.

- Dove è l'ospedale più vicino? (DOH-veh eh lohs-peh-DAH-leh pee-oo vee-CHEE-noh?) - Where is the nearest hospital?

- Mi sono perso/a. (mee SOH-noh PEHR-soh/ah) - I'm lost.

- Parla inglese? (PAHR-lah een-GLEH-zeh?) - Do you speak English?

- Non capisco. (non kah-PEES-koh) - I don't understand.

CURRENCY, BANKING AND SHOPPING

HOURS

The currency used in Milan, like in the rest of Italy and many European Union nations, is the Euro (€). Coins exist in denominations of 1, 2, 5, 10, 20, and 50 cents, and 1 and 2 euros. Banknotes are available in 5, 10, 20, 50, 100, 200, and 500 euros. It's wise to bring a combination of cash and cards throughout your stay, since smaller places may not take cards for little sums.

Banking

ATMs and Banks: ATMs (Bancomat in Italian) are extensively distributed across Milan, allowing a quick option to withdraw cash 24/7. They accept most foreign debit and credit cards, however it's recommended to advise your bank of your vacation intentions to prevent any bans on your cards. Banks are normally open from Monday to Friday, 8:30 AM to 1:30 PM and again from 2:30 PM to 4:00 PM, however, hours might vary.

Money Exchange: While you may exchange money in banks, post offices, and some travel companies, it's often more cost-effective to withdraw euros from ATMs. If you need to convert money, currency exchange offices (cambio) are available at the airport, rail stations, and other tourist sites, but be cautious of conversion rates and costs.

Shopping Hours

General Hours: Shopping in Milan is a lovely experience, with hours that accommodate both early birds and night owls. Most stores are open from 10:00 AM to 7:30 PM, Monday through Saturday. Some could shut for lunch from about 1:00 PM to 3:30 PM, particularly smaller, family-run enterprises.

Late Nights and Sundays: Thursday is generally a late shopping night, with many shops remaining open until 9:00 PM or later. In recent years, Sunday shopping has grown increasingly widespread, especially in the city center and tourist regions, with businesses operating from approximately midday until 7:00 PM or later.

Department Stores and Malls: Larger department stores, shopping malls, and outlets could have extended hours, often from 10:00 AM to 9:00 PM, including Sundays. The Galleria Vittorio Emanuele II, one of the world's oldest shopping malls, situated near the Duomo, is a must-visit for its gorgeous architecture and luxurious boutiques.

Seasonal Sales: If you're searching for savings, keep an eye out for seasonal sales (saldi), which normally occur in January and July. During certain occasions, you may discover big savings on apparel, accessories, and more.

Tips for Shopping

-**Tax-Free Purchasing**: Non-EU citizens may profit from tax-free purchasing of products to be exported. Look for businesses displaying a "Tax-Free Shopping" sign and ask for a tax refund form while completing your purchase.

- **Quality and Authenticity**: Milan is famed for its high-quality products, notably fashion and design items. To assure authenticity, particularly when buying designer products, purchase at reputed outlets or directly at brand boutiques.

- Local goods: Beyond fashion, Milan and the neighboring Lombardy area provide wonderful local goods, including wines, cheeses, and artisanal crafts, making for distinctive souvenirs.

ITINERARY

1-DAY QUICK TOUR

Morning:

- Duomo di Milano: Start your day early at Milan's stunning cathedral. Take time to explore its gothic architecture and, if possible, climb the rooftop for a spectacular perspective of the city.

- Galleria Vittorio Emanuele II: Walk around this luxurious retail gallery to marvel at its architecture and maybe take a quick coffee in one of the old cafés.

Afternoon:

- Sforza fortress: Explore this Renaissance fortress and its museums, featuring Michelangelo's final work, the Rondanini Pietà.

- Parco Sempione: Enjoy a leisurely walk through this verdant paradise behind the castle, a fantastic area for a picnic or relaxation.

Evening:

- Navigli District: Conclude your day with the bustling Navigli district. This district is famed for its canal system developed by Leonardo da Vinci and is an excellent setting for supper and drinks.

3-DAY CULTURAL DEEP DIVE

Day 1: Historic Milan

- Morning: Visit the Duomo and Galleria Vittorio Emanuele II, as above.

- Afternoon: Explore the Teatro alla Scala and its museum. If feasible, reserve a ticket for a performance.

- Evening: Dine in the Brera neighborhood, noted for its bohemian air, and visit the Brera Art Gallery if time permits.

Day 2: Art and Design

- Morning: Start with the Pinacoteca di Brera for a thorough dive into Renaissance art.

- Afternoon: Visit the Museo del Novecento for contemporary Italian art, followed by a visit to the Triennale di Milano, which focuses on Italian design.

- Evening: Explore the Isola neighborhood for supper, noted for its dynamic nightlife and modern architecture.

Day 3: Leonardo da Vinci's Milan

- Morning: Visit Santa Maria delle Grazie to witness The Last Supper (planning is essential).

- Afternoon: Explore the Leonardo da Vinci National Museum of Science and Technology.

-Evening: Enjoy a lunch in the Corso Como district, followed by a stroll to the contemporary Piazza Gae Aulenti.

5-DAY COMPREHENSIVE EXPLORATION

Day 1 & 2: Follow the 2-day schedule above, exploring old Milan and its art and design legacy.

Day 3:

- Dedicate this day to touring Leonardo da Vinci's Milan as specified in the 3-day program.

Day 4: Milanese Lifestyle

- Morning: Shop at the Quadrilatero della Moda, Milan's high-end fashion sector.

- Afternoon: Relax on the Giardini Pubblici, then explore the neighboring Natural History Museum or the PAC (Contemporary Art Pavilion).

- Evening: Have supper in the Porta Venezia district, providing varied gastronomic alternatives.

Day 5: Day Trip

- Option 1: Lake Como: Take a train to Como and spend the day touring the quaint villages surrounding the lake, having a boat trip, and appreciating the gorgeous countryside.

- Option 2: Bergamo: Discover the historic splendor of Bergamo Alta, savor its local food, and wander along its Venetian walls with magnificent views.

CONCLUSION

In the pages of this Milan travel guide, we've walked together through the sweeping metropolitan elegance of Italy's fashion city, from the grand Duomo that pierces the sky to the tranquil waters of the Navigli canals at sunset. It's been a tour not only through locations but through feelings, where every cobblestone street and secret piazza has whispered tales of ages past, beckoning us to become part of Milan's continuing story.

Our joint voyage has been interrupted with amazing moments: the first view of the Last Supper, the afternoon light throwing shadows over Sforza Castle, and the taste of real risotto alla Milanese at a lively local trattoria. These encounters, unique in their depth, have built memories that remain, like the lingering tones of a violin in the enormous auditorium of Teatro alla Scala.

Alongside these recollections, we've compiled practical suggestions to traverse the city's complexity with ease, from learning the art of the aperitivo to finding calm in the city's beautiful parks. Our book has attempted to provide you with the information to explore Milan with confidence, fitting smoothly into the fabric of this vibrant city.

As we complete this chapter, I express my sincerest thanks for allowing me to be your guide. Milan, with its incomparable combination of art, history, and modernity, provides unlimited chances for exploration, and I invite you to continue exploring its depths. The city, ever-evolving but unwavering in its tradition, awaits your return with open arms and fresh mysteries to uncover.

May this book be the beginning of your love affair with Milan, prompting you to return, explore, and dream. Milan is not simply a destination; it's a voyage of the heart, an invitation to uncover beauty in the commonplace and the spectacular.

So, I leave you with a call to action: journey out with open eyes and an open heart. Let Milan's energy inspire your journeys, wherever they may take you. And remember, every voyage is a chance to discover not only new vistas but something fundamental inside ourselves.

With heartfelt thoughts and wishes for your future trips,

Made in the USA
Las Vegas, NV
28 September 2024

95927690R00075